Every
MOM
*should have
a book
like this...*

Other Titles in This Series:

*Every Daughter Should Have a Book like This
to Remind Her How Wonderful She Is*

*Every Sister Should Have a Book like This
to Let Her Know What a Blessing She Is*

*Every Son Should Have a Book like This
Filled with Wishes, Love, and
Encouragement*

All writings are by Douglas Pagels except as noted.

Library of Congress Control Number: 2007907328
ISBN: 978-1-59842-312-9

◘ and Blue Mountain Press are registered in U.S. Patent and Trademark Office. Certain trademarks are used under license.

Acknowledgments appear on page 72.

Printed in China.
First Printing: 2008

♲ This book is printed on recycled paper.

This book is printed on fine quality, laid embossed, 80 lb. paper. This paper has been specially produced to be acid free (neutral pH) and contains no groundwood or unbleached pulp. It conforms with the requirements of the American National Standards Institute, Inc., so as to ensure that this book will last and be enjoyed by future generations.

Blue Mountain Arts, Inc.
P.O. Box 4549, Boulder, Colorado 80306

Every
MOM
*should have
a book
like this*

*filled with
love and
appreciation*

Douglas Pagels

Blue Mountain Press™
Boulder, Colorado

Contents

Remember What Jennifer Said...

My mother was my strength and my discipline. She made it possible for me to follow all of my dreams and become what I am today.

— Jennifer Lopez

This Is for You, Mom...

You're an amazing, remarkable woman whose example guides me, whose wisdom always points me in the right direction, and whose love I carry with me through every turn in the road.

The things you have given me through the years of my life have been some of the most priceless treasures any person could have ever received.

And I thank you with all my heart for giving them to me.

Mom, I want you to know why I love you so much

Do you know what you are, Mom? You're one of the most wonderful people in the whole world.

I really mean that. The older I get, the more I understand how rare it is to be blessed with a mother like you. You're unique in so many ways, and there are very few things in life that even come close to bringing me as much happiness as you do.

You never cease to amaze me. There are so many moments when I am quietly in awe of you... of the joy you inspire, of the serenity you share, and of all the great things that just seem to naturally be a part of you. When I stop and think of everything you are, it opens my eyes to all the wonderful qualities about you. I see goodness and kindness there. I see compassion and understanding...

And I never fail to see a twinkle in your eyes... a gentle reminder to me that I am in the company of someone who has a big heart and a beautiful ability to make each day a good one.

I'll always think the world of you. I'll cherish all the memories and appreciate the closeness and be eternally grateful for everything.

So please... don't ever forget:

I think you are one of the most precious people this world will ever be blessed with.

Remember What Katie Said...

My mother has always been there for me, and I appreciate and enjoy her even more every day.

— Katie Couric

You're the Best

This is for the mother I love, for the one who has cared all these years, but who has never heard enough about how much I care.

This is for the one who has helped me through all my childhood fears and failures, and turned all that she could into successes and dreams.

This is for the woman who is a wonderful example of what more people ought to be.

This is for the person whose devotion to her family is marked by strength and sacrifice, and whose love of life, farsighted guidance, and everyday wisdom make more sense to me now than nearly any other thing I've learned.

If you never knew how much I love you, I want you to know it now.

And if you never knew how much I appreciate and admire you... let me just say that I think you're the best mother any child ever had.

Remember What Barack Said...

I know that she was the kindest, most generous spirit I have ever known, and that what is best in me I owe to her.

— Barack Obama

There are so many moments when I wish you knew how much you matter to me, and how much I thank you for being such a wonderful mother...

*If there is happiness in my heart,
it's because you helped put
it there.*

*If there is gentleness in my beliefs,
it's because you showed me how
to care.*

*If there is understanding in my
thinking, it's because you shared
your wisdom.*

If there is a rainbow over my shoulder, it's because of your outlook and your vision.

If there is knowledge that I can reach out — and really can make some dreams come true — it's because I learned from the best teacher of all. I learned from you...

In the times of my life, whether we are near or far, please remember that there could never be any mother more wonderful... than you.

Remember What Meredith Said...

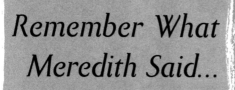

She instilled in her children such strength of character and dignity and "do the right thing." Her qualities, they're sort of the simple ones that mean the most.

— Meredith Vieira

You Are One Amazing Lady

Mom, I want you to know that you're one amazing lady.

You are so good to the people in your life. So considerate and caring. When you give, it's easy to see that it comes straight from the heart... and it gives everyone around you the gift of a nicer world to live in.

I hope you'll never forget how much I treasure just being in this world with you. And I love knowing that everyone else feels the same way I do. To your family, you are dearly loved and truly the best.

You are such a deserving person. And I really hope that all of your days are as beautiful and as bright... as the ones you inspire in other people's lives.

Remember What Sheryl Said...

All my life, I have been able to rely on my mother to be my closest confidant. I treasure most our quiet moments talking over coffee, in the late morning, at home. Her compassion and wonderful ability to laugh at life's little foibles have been a great inspiration to me.

— Sheryl Crow

A Mother Is...

A mother is life at its best. She understands. She goes a million miles out of her way just to lend a hand. She brings you smiles when a smile is exactly what you needed. She listens, and she hears what is said in the spaces between the words. A mother cares, and she lets you know you're in her prayers...

A mother can guide you, inspire you, comfort you, and light up your life. She understands your moods and nurtures your needs. She lovingly knows just what would help make things right.

A mother always knows the perfect thing to do. She can make your whole day just by saying something that no one else could have said.

Sometimes you feel like the two of you share a secret language that others can't tune in to.

When your feelings come from deep inside and need to be spoken to someone you don't have to hide from, you share those innermost feelings with your mother. When good news comes, she is the first one you turn to. When feelings overflow and tears need to fall, a mother helps you through it all...

A mother brings sunlight into your life. She warms your world with her presence, whether she is far away or close by your side. A mother is a wonderful gift, one that brings so much happiness, and she's a treasure that money can't buy.

Remember What Sean Said...

When I look back, that is just what she gave... the reassurance that we were loved and that we mattered. This was the most valuable essence, the roots that live and grow forever inside you. She truly was a wonderful mother and friend.

— Sean Hepburn Ferrer

Mom, you are enormously thanked and endlessly appreciated

There are a few absolute gems in this world. They are the people who make a tremendous difference in other people's lives... with the smiles they give, the blessings they share, and the way they warm the hearts of everyone around them.

Those rare and remarkable people are so deserving of every hope and happiness. They are the people who are incredibly unique, enormously thanked, and endlessly appreciated for everything they do.

And one of those wonderful, deserving, and one-of-a-kind people is most definitely... you.

Remember What Kelly Said...

The word mom *embodies a person who not only is a friend, support system, and mentor; she is someone that her children can rely on at any hour of the day....*

She is the greatest person you know, the person you aspire to be the most like, and the person who will forever offer her unwavering support.

— Kelly Ripa

I know I'll never be able to truly thank you... for all the years of loving grace you have blessed me with, and for the gifts of keeping me in your heart and for making my happiness so complete.

One of the most special places in my heart will always be saved for you.

You... the one person I can always talk to; the one person who understands.

You... for making me laugh in the rain; for helping me shoulder my troubles.

You... for loving me in spite of myself, and always putting me back on my feet again.

You... for giving me someone to believe in; someone who lets me know that there really is goodness and kindness and laughter and love in the world.

You... for being one of the best parts of my life, and proving it over and over again.

Mom, you deserve to know that...

It takes someone special to do what you do. It takes someone rare and remarkable to make her family's world and the lives of everyone around her nicer, brighter, and more beautiful. It takes someone who has a big heart and a caring soul. It takes someone who's living proof of how precious a person can be.

It takes someone... just like you.

Remember What Carrie Said...

I know that when the going gets rough I can go to my mother. She will comfort me and take my side and nurture me back to where I can nurture myself. Knowing that my mother is in my corner doesn't make me feel as though I'm in a corner at all. It makes the world a friendlier place to be.

— Carrie Fisher

To the Best Mom of All

If a star were to fall in the sky tonight,
and I could make a wish... the one thing
I would ask for is that you would never
forget that you're the best mother there is.

You have helped me hold on to so many
memories of our special yesterdays, and
you have helped me touch tomorrow...
just by loving me and encouraging me to
go after my hopes and dreams and to do
what I can to make them come true.

You have given me the perfectly precious gift of your love, and I want you to know that I value it more highly than any treasure on this earth. I hope you know how much I appreciate everything you do.

I'm glad you love me so much.

I love you so much, too.

Remember What Lance Said...

How do you adequately express gratitude for the gifts from a parent? I've tried in various ways to tell her thank you over the years. Only once did I come close to succeeding, and even then it was an awkward attempt....

"I want you to know how much I love my life," I said, "and how much I love you for giving it to me."

At this writing, I wish I could find better, more eloquent words with which to thank her. But I don't seem able to improve on that very simple statement, uttered in gratitude: I love this life — and I love and appreciate her for giving it to me.

— Lance Armstrong

There are so many days when I wish I could find a way... to sincerely and dearly thank you. You brought me into the world and did everything you could to make it my very own heaven on earth.

Even in the times when I may have caused you concern, you never gave up on me. I always felt you there; I always knew I was in your prayers and in your heart's warmest wishes.

I want to say "thanks" to you, Mom, for being the finest, kindest person I know. Your lessons are with me, in some meaningful way, every day. When I think of how much you have cared for me, whether I deserved it or not, I am simply in awe of your generosity.

Your wise words have guided me through so much, and you have touched my heart more deeply than anyone else. Thank you for being an encouraging soul who lifts me up on the strength of your belief in me and on the wings of what you see in me...

*You are everything that love could ever...
and should ever... be. You're my anchor,
Mom, and my rock and my beacon of light
in any times of difficulty in my life.*

*I feel like I can turn to you and talk to you
about anything. And I wish I could thank
you... for absolutely everything.*

Remember What Judy Said...

I am so lucky that my mother has turned out to be my close friend, someone I can talk to about everything....

That is about as good as it could get, and I got it. I am one lucky daughter.

— Judy Collins

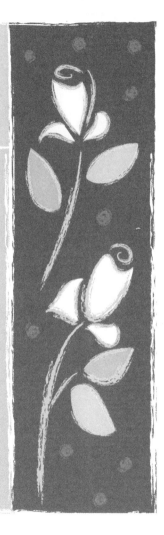

"I Love You, Mom"

What can you say to someone who has always been one of the most essential parts of your world; someone who took you by the hand when you were little and helped to show the way?

What do you say to someone who stood by to help you grow, providing love, strength, and support so you could become the person you are today?

What can you say to let her know that she's the best there is and that you hope you've inherited some of her wisdom and her strength?

What words would you say if you ever got the chance?

Maybe you just say "I love you, Mom..." and hope she understands.

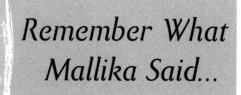

Remember What Mallika Said...

When I think about what kind of mother I would like to be, I have to look only at my own mother as a shining example.

My mother is the embodiment of love, compassion, and caring.... She is driven by the love she has for others, and she goes to extreme lengths to quietly make sure that those she loves are taken care of.

— *Mallika Chopra*

How Blessed I Am to Have You in My Life

You always let me know how much you love me... with your words, your concern, your hugs, and your sweet hopes for everything I do.

You help me put my life back together every time things fall apart. You like me no matter what... even when I have a hard time feeling good about myself...

You see beyond the surface side of me, and you know that there are lots of special things about me that others don't always take the time to discover.

You give me a beautiful glimpse of what it must be like for a person to have a guardian angel in their life.

Thanks, Mom, for your unbelievable help and support, for your caring and your constant love. I feel like my life has been very blessed, and I'm so lucky to have you in it.

And I truly believe that the best mother in the world is the one who is reading these words... right this very minute.

Your love is what sees me through more things than you'll ever realize. I cherish our closeness, just like I've treasured every generous, giving, understanding, and supportive thing you've ever done for me. The list goes on and on, and I'm not sure I could ever count all the things you've done that have made a difference to my heart and to my happiness.

Remember What Queen Latifah Said...

My mother always told me how smart, beautiful, and talented I was. In her mind, there was nothing I couldn't do. When I wanted to learn the drums and guitar, she paid for lessons. When I entered talent shows, she sat in the front row. When I played basketball, she was there, cheering the loudest. And when I got into trouble... she talked with me and she prayed for me. She never limited me. My mother believed in me before I even believed in myself. And because of that, no one can shake my confidence now.

— Queen Latifah

Now that I'm older, I see just as much with my heart as I do with my eyes. Now that I understand things a little more, I'm better at being able to realize the inherent value in your smiles, in your words, and in the treasure of every single way you show your love.

Now I know why you're so important to me. You have believed in me and encouraged me all my life. You teach me so much and provide for me so well. You have sacrificed in your lifetime to make so many things better in mine.

Now I know why you're so amazing to me. You do anything and everything any child could ever ask a mother to do, and then — as if that wasn't enough — your eyes smile my way and you always seem to say, "Is there anything I can do for you?"

You know what, Mom? There is something you can do. You can lovingly remember that there are so many times when the one thing that always and forever sees me through is just knowing... that I have the most wonderful mother in all the world... in you.

Remember What John Said...

My beautiful, sweet mother and I would sit on the front porch of our house... and count the stars in the sky. We'd have long talks that only a young son and his mother could have and, before we went into the house, she'd always give me a big hug and a kiss, and tell me how much she loved me.

I never fail to think of her when I look at the nighttime starry sky.

— John Lappen

In the course of a person's lifetime, there are so many prayers that get whispered and so many hopes that fill the heart. There are wishing stars that spend their entire evenings listening to all the things we long for.

I have said those prayers and had those hopes and chatted with more than my share of stars in the sky.

I always feel that if I ask and believe and wish well enough, some things are bound to turn out right.

But in all my prayers and wishes and hopes, I couldn't have asked for a blessing more wonderful than you in my life.

What a Difference
a Mom Makes

A mother who's there for you is one of the nicest things anyone can have. There are special words of encouragement that only she can give. There are certain words of strength and understanding that only she can share. There are lessons to pass along and there is wisdom to impart.

There are times that can only be described as "mom moments"... when things need to be heard from her outlook, filtered through her experience, and expressed straight from her heart. There are wonderful memories to make, bonds to be absolutely sure of, and so many smiles to inspire.

It's one of the nicest things in the whole wide world. It's something more precious than any treasure I could ever find. And it's a blessing I have had all my life, but one that I value more and more with every passing year, every thankful memory, and every hope in my heart.

What is it?

It's having a mother like you.

Remember What Katherine Said...

Everybody knows that a good mother gives her children a feeling of trust and stability. She is their earth. She is the one they can count on for the things that matter most of all.

— Katherine Butler Hathaway

What Mothers Are
to Their Children

A place they can always find comfort.
A hand they can reach out and clasp.
Eyes they can look at and trust.
A heart that understands.

To their children, mothers are
someone they can lean on
and learn from.

They are a source of wisdom
and loving advice.
A million memories in the making.
A precious companion on the path of life.

A door that is always open.
A caring, gentle hug.
A time that is devoted
to family alone.
A constant reflection of love.

Remember What Sidney Said...

She communicated very eloquently in the way that she cared for me, the way her spirit hovers over me to this day, her presence always around me, guiding me in ways I'm still trying to understand.

— Sidney Poitier

All the wonderful, caring qualities so necessary in a mother...

A gentleness so gentle, a strength that few could match, the kind of understanding that no one else could even begin to provide, a steady hand to hold on the journey through life... the knowing, the growing, the holding close, the letting go, the reflections of love in every glance...

All the wonderful qualities so necessary in a mother... are the things you possess in such abundance.

When I Say
"I Love You, Mom..."

I'm really trying to say so much more.

I'm trying to find a way to tell one of the kindest, most understanding, and big-hearted people in the world that she is more wonderful than my words will ever be able to say.

I'm trying to express a thanks for the happiness I get when I feel such gratitude for our family bond... a bond that is stronger and sweeter than anything else will ever be.

There are a lot of things I want you to remember, but there are two things in particular that I absolutely have to be certain of...

Even if you don't get to hear it all the time, I have to be sure that you know, every single day... how much you're appreciated and how dearly you're loved.

You are a very special part of my life.

You are a kind of "touchstone" for me. You're a source of reflection, someone whom I can talk with, listen to, or just think of. And the next thing I know, I see the way more clearly. I understand myself a lot better. And I find myself appreciating what a unique and wonderful person you are... more and more as time goes on.

Remember What Reba Said...

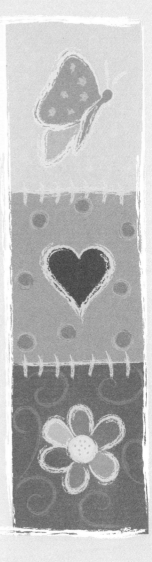

There's just nothing stronger or more lasting than a good mama's influence, that special sense of security when she's around that you can still pull close to you for comfort when she's physically far away.

— Reba McEntire

May Your Life Be Filled with All These Things

*A little more joy,
a little less stress,
a lot more
recognition of
your wonderfulness.*

Abundance in your life,
blessings in your days,
dreams that come true,
and hopes that stay.

A rainbow on the horizon,
an angel by your side...
and everything
that could ever bring
a smile to your life.

And Remember
What I Said...

Mom, if you could see yourself reflected in my eyes, you would see someone who makes my heart just smile inside. You would catch a glimpse of somebody who has been such a wonderful influence on my life and who keeps on making a beautiful difference in my days.

— *Douglas Pagels*

If you could hear the words I would love to share, you would be able to listen to a special tribute to you, one that sings your praises and speaks of an unending gratitude and describes how much I'll always appreciate you.

And if you could imagine one of the nicest presents anyone could ever receive, you would begin to understand what your presence in my life has meant to me.

ACKNOWLEDGMENTS

We gratefully acknowledge the permission granted by the following authors, publishers, and authors' representatives to reprint poems or excerpts from their publications.

Little, Brown and Co., Inc., for "My mother has always been..." by Katie Couric from LIFE WITH MOTHER, by the editors of *Life* Magazine. Copyright © 1995 by Time, Inc. Introduction copyright © 1995 by Katie Couric. Reprinted by permission of Little, Brown and Co., Inc. All rights reserved.

Harry N. Abrams, NY, for "My mother was my strength..." by Jennifer Lopez, "All my life, I have been able to..." by Sheryl Crow, and "I know that when..." by Carrie Fisher from HOLLYWOOD MOMS by Joyce Ostin. Copyright © 2001 by Joyce Ostin. All rights reserved.

Three Rivers Press, an imprint of Random House, Inc., for "I know that she was the kindest..." from DREAMS FROM MY FATHER by Barack Obama. Copyright © 1995, 2004 by Barack Obama. All rights reserved.

Jeanne Marie Laskas for "She instilled in her children..." by Meredith Vieira from "When Is Meredith Vieira an Open Book?" Originally published in *Ladies' Home Journal* by Jeanne Marie Laskas (May 2007). Copyright © 2007 by Jeanne Marie Laskas. All rights reserved.

Atria, an imprint of Simon & Schuster Adult Publishing Group, for "When I look back, that is just what..." from AUDREY HEPBURN: AN ELEGANT SPIRIT by Sean Hepburn Ferrer. Copyright © 2003 by Sean Hepburn Ferrer. All rights reserved.

Hyperion for "The word *mom*..." by Kelly Ripa from I LOVE YOU, MOM! Foreword by Kelly Ripa. Copyright © 2003 by My Poppy, Inc. Reprinted by permission of Hyperion. All rights reserved.

Broadway Books, a division of Random House, Inc., for "How do you adequately express..." by Lance Armstrong from NO MOUNTAIN HIGH ENOUGH by Linda Armstrong Kelly. Copyright © 2005 by Linda Armstrong Kelly. All rights reserved.

Jeremy P. Tarcher, an imprint of Penguin Group (USA), Inc., for "I am so lucky that..." from "Youth, Light, and Memory" from SANITY AND GRACE by Judy Collins. Copyright © 2003 by Judy Collins. All rights reserved.

Rodale, Inc., Emmaus, PA 18098, www.rodalestore.com, for "When I think about what kind..." from 100 PROMISES TO MY BABY by Mallika Chopra. Copyright © 2005 by Mallika Chopra. All rights reserved.

William Morrow, a division of HarperCollins Publishers, for "My mother always told me..." from LADIES FIRST by Queen Latifah and Karen Hunter. Copyright © 1999 by Queen Latifah, Inc. All rights reserved.

Fireside, an imprint of Simon & Schuster Adult Publishing Group, for "My beautiful, sweet mother and I..." by John Lappen from 100 WAYS TO BEAT THE BLUES by Tanya Tucker and Friends. Copyright © 2005 by Tanya Tucker. All rights reserved.

The Feminist Press at the City University of New York, www.feministpress.org, for "Everybody knows that a good mother..." from THE LITTLE LOCKSMITH: A MEMOIR by Katherine Butler Hathaway. Copyright 1942, 1943 by Coward-McCann, Inc., renewed © 1974 by Warren H. Butler. All rights reserved.

HarperCollins Publishers for "She communicated very eloquently..." from THE MEASURE OF A MAN: A SPIRITUAL AUTOBIOGRAPHY by Sidney Poitier. Copyright © 2000 by Sidney Poitier. All rights reserved.

Bantam Books, a division of Random House, Inc., for "There's just nothing stronger or more..." from COMFORT FROM A COUNTRY QUILT by Reba McEntire. Copyright © 1999 by Reba McEntire. All rights reserved.

A careful effort has been made to trace the ownership of selections used in this anthology in order to obtain permission to reprint copyrighted material and give proper credit to the copyright owners. If any error or omission has occurred, it is completely inadvertent, and we would like to make corrections in future editions provided that written notification is made to the publisher:

BLUE MOUNTAIN ARTS, INC., P.O. Box 4549, Boulder, Colorado 80306.